SARK SEAFOOD

SARK SEAFOOD

GOOD FOOD IN THE CHARMING ISLAND OF SARK

The Aval du Creux Hotel

SARK SEAFOOD

RECIPES FROM

THE AVAL DU CREUX HOTEL
SARK

CONTENTS

The Head Chef

INTRODUCTION

INTRODUCTION TO SARK AND
THE AVAL DU CREUX HOTEL

Journeying to a small island by sea is a special experience and since Sark has no airstrip, there is no other way of getting there. Whether crossing the nine miles of open water from Guernsey in the stubby service boat, the Bon Marin, or winging up from France by twin-hulled ferry, arrival at Maseline Harbour is full of bustle. Mail, papers and luggage are handed briskly up the steps and loaded onto waiting tractors. Passengers leave the quay through a tunnel in the cliff to find the toast rack waiting, a tractor-drawn bus that will carry them up the hill through a wooded valley to the village above.

Those preferring a more leisured pace can wander up the footpath through the bracken slopes and woods to emerge opposite the Aval du Creux Hotel. Either way, the bouncy bus ride or the steep walk up, you are instantly immersed in the Sark experience, best described as physically engaging. Because there are only unmade roads and no cars, getting about means either walking or bicycling; without any streetlights or background clutter, nights can be truly dark and filled with stars and there are the ever-present sounds of the sea.

Footpath leading up Harbour Hill

Sark Lighthouse with the Maseline Harbour and Sark ferry

*Preparing the
Hotel restaurant*

The Aval du Creux Hotel and Restaurant is a handsome granite building, its entrance guarded by a magnificent horse chestnut tree. It was the traditional Sark tenement house on one of the original farms settled by Helier de Carteret and his colonisers from Jersey in 1565. Armed with Letters Patent from Elizabeth I, he sailed over with forty families, all bearing a musket to defend their share of the island against whoever came, freebooters, raiders, the French, or any other claimants. Although a modest farm cottage with a few outbuildings, the Aval tenement was in a favoured position being directly above the all-important Creux Harbour built in the 1570's. (The name is a corruption of Avant du Creux, Above the Creux, aval means below).

In 1834 a ten-year period of silver mining in Little Sark brought Cornish miners, a resident doctor and extra money generally to the island. Several Sark families improved or rebuilt their houses and the Aval became a substantial two-storey tenement house in 1841. By 1950 it was being run as a guest house and tea garden, serving home-made cakes and cream teas to the first post-war tourists.

It has been a hotel ever since, gradually being renovated and extended to provide modern comfort with old-fashioned standards of hospitality and flexibility, using Channel Island granite and Welsh slate, employing local stonemasons and craftsmen to give the hotel its present look of traditional and enduring solidity. Built on a south facing slope, it comprises several beautiful stone buildings and an intriguing round Norman tower. The internationally renowned restaurant overlooks the pool and gardens and is large enough to cater for weddings and corporate events but there are smaller more intimate rooms where guests can unwind with a book or laptop.

Relaxing in the garden under an ancient pear tree, it is hard to believe that traffic jams and airport check-in queues are only a few miles away. Here all is the very essence of peacefulness and the sound of the church bell half a mile away or the honking of a few geese from across the headland only accentuate that charm. Idling by the pool you might catch the distant drone of an aircraft but Sark does not allow over-flying below two thousand feet. You may even hear the French ferry reversing out of the harbour, but only faintly and largely drowned out by birdsong. There are tractors for general carting and farm work but the speed limit is ten miles per hour and they must be off the road by 10 pm. Not so the horses, which may be heard clip-clopping along quite late at night with a carriage full of sleepy diners.

Sark's climate is undeniably more benign than that of the UK, milder with more hours of sunshine - perfect for breakfast out of doors on a summer morning. All meals at the Aval can be taken al fresco, either in the garden, by the pool or under a generous awning on the terrace. Dining by lamplight outside gives you a chance to watch the tiny pipistrelle bats flitting among the trees at dusk.

The Hotel pool and terrace

SARK

For yachtsmen cruising the Channel Islands, lunch at the Aval while waiting for a favourable tide has always been popular. Boat-owners can anchor in any of the sheltered bays or pick up a mooring in Havre Gosselin before tramping across the island to enjoy a leg of Sark lamb with spring vegetables. Hedonists might opt for an unhurried carriage ride around the island, sightseeing at two and a quarter miles an hour, perhaps taking in a stroll through the Seigneurie Gardens, and finishing up with a lobster salad at the Aval - quite a seductive prospect.

Sark's shellfish is second to none. The three-mile fishing limit is guarded by stringent laws aimed at protecting stocks and ensuring a fishing industry for tomorrow. Export of Sark scallops is forbidden - they must all be sold on the island. Perhaps the tractor puttering up Harbour Hill at tea-time is delivering scallops to the hotel for the chef's appraisal, dived at slack water that afternoon and as yet unshucked. Lobsters caught daily in the cold clear waters are in the kitchen in a couple of hours. Crab must be trapped in traditional pots, no parlour pots allowed, and during the early weeks of the season there is the sweet meat of spider crab.

The waters of Sark are said to be too clean for mussels and oysters but there are extensive oyster beds in Jersey just a few miles to the south and Aval's exacting chef has easy access to those markets for the best and freshest.

Local fishermen ensure plentiful supplies of bass, turbot, brill and pollock, caught on the banks and shoals around the island. Sark's fishing boats are inshore craft, lacking freezing facilities aboard and not designed to stay at sea overnight, so the fish is up the hill and into the kitchen within hours of catching. Guernsey has a much larger fishing fleet and supplies of deep water fish are only hours away.

Opposite: Sark fisherman and lobster

Road to the west

Sark may be small, three miles by one and a half at its widest point, but it does have an extraordinarily varied landscape. From seaward the cliffs can seem barren and rather sombre but as you approach the island, deep gullies and bays open out to reveal themselves as sheltered coves with wooded paths or steps down for access. The island is a deeply indented plateau and the Mill, built in 1571 in the middle of the island at its highest point of 356 feet, is surrounded by small fields and sweet meadows, thick flowering hedges and a great arch of sky.

Standing knee-deep in buttercups are the famous Guernsey cows, crossed with Angus or Hereford if being bred for beef. Unsurprisingly, the meat is superb and farmers can sell all they raise - hardly a food mile involved. Free-range Sark pork is traditionally reared at the Seigneurie Farm and results in extremely tender and delicious meat.

Aval du Creux Restaurant buys its lamb from the west coast - the west coast of Sark that is. These are animals that have grazed on the cotils, the fields just inside the cliff tops on the edge of the island where they are sheltered from the salty winds by gorse-scented hedges. They simply could not be better quality.

West coast cliffs

AS SEEN FROM FRANCE

The Hotel bar and wine

The French call the Channel Islands "les Iles Anglo-Normandes" and their proximity to France certainly lends a special flavour to the islands; place names, family names, the sight of the Normandy coastline which, on a clear day, seems so close that the waiters can almost be seen setting out the tables for lunch. It does also mean that those lovely soft cheeses reach Sark in the best of health.

The island has a thriving milk industry and practically no milk is imported even in high season. Little Sark, too, has its own herd of purebred Guernsey cattle. Until very recently, cows tethered near the lighthouse were hand-milked and the farm nearby still sells unpasteurized milk to its regular customers.

Sark cream has to be seen and tasted to be believed and makes ambrosial ice-cream. After a scramble down to Derrible Bay to visit the sea-caves or an afternoon spent bodysurfing at Grande Gréve, a Sark cream tea - scones, thick golden cream and strawberry jam is the ideal restorative.

The sight, and sound, of hens scratching in the warm dust of the poultry run is quite common as many people keep a few chickens. Eggs can be bought "off the hedge", fresh, free-range and probably organic, while one chicken farm supplies the hotels and restaurants. Sark butter, very deep yellow and made in the traditional round shape, is available in the local shops. At the annual Sark Garden and Farm Produce Show the dairy section of butter, eggs, milk and cream is keenly contested; there is no class for low-fat spreads.

Buying island vegetables, meat and dairy products, Sark-caught shellfish, lobster and crab, it's not surprising that the chef produces such delicious and appetizing dishes. He works with very sound ingredients. He is also particularly fortunate in that the hotel's extensive wine list features many good wines to compliment his dishes.

Good food and wine deserve keen appetites and there is something about Sark's exceptionally pure air that stimulates the palate and adds greatly to the pleasures of eating well. Following an afternoon exploring the silver mines in Little Sark or snorkelling at low tide around the fascinating Autelets rocks, the rewards of a fine cuisine are particularly appreciated. Even the gentler diversions of Sark, such as settling back into the springy turf of a headland to watch the sea or simply read a book, will give you a pleasing appetite.

What could be a more delightful end to a day on Sark than to take an after-dinner stroll out to the Pilcher monument on the west coast to watch the setting sun, before sauntering back along honeysuckle scented lanes to enjoy a sloe gin on the terrace at Aval du Creux?

Courgette cultivation on the Island

THE CHEF & FISH

GARY THOMPSON IS HEAD CHEF OF THE AVAL DU CREUX HOTEL, SARK.

Gary Thompson has worked at the Aval du Creux for the last ten years. He now lives full time in Sark with his wife and family. "In Sark we are working predominantly with fresh produce, about 50 per cent of which is grown on the island in what are more or less organic conditions. I also love working with fresh sea food and here I know exactly how fresh it is, unlike many other places where fish has to be shipped in." In fact, when he is not at work, Gary can often be found out at sea with local fishermen helping catch the fish that will be served in the hotel restaurant that night. "You can't get fresher than that," he says.

A Guide to Quality: Absolute freshness is essential if the best is to be obtained from any fish dish, both in flavour and nourishment. Stale fish are not only un-appetising but can also be the cause of digestive disorders or even poisoning. Nowadays with quick freezing, the bulk of the fish reaches the markets frozen and if the fish was frozen whilst fresh and it is used immediately after defrosting, it will be almost the equal of fresh fish. "I have to say though that when I get my fresh fish from the locals it is still wiggling, so no worries there!"

The following are some tests which can be applied to determine the freshness of your fish:

1   The eyes should be bright and full, not sunken

2   The gills should be bright, pinkish red in colour

3   The flesh must be firm and springy

4   Scales, if any should be plentiful, firm and should not come off when the fish is handled

5   The fish should have a pleasant salty smell

Sure signs and indications of stale fish are:

1   An unpleasant odour which increases with time

2   Limp flesh retaining the imprint of ones fingers

3   Sunken eyes

4   Gills dull and discoloured.

The quality is also determined by the condition of the skin, which should be shining and of good colour. The flesh of white fish should

be really white, not yellowish. The fish should feel heavy in relating to its size with the flesh being plump and springy.

Brecqhou and The Gouliot Headland

THE RECIPES

STARTERS

BRUSCHETTA
WITH GARLIC BRUSHED CIABATTA
24

HOT CRAB AND BOURSIN TARTLETS
26

MOULES MARINIÈRE
28

OYSTERS A LA FLORENTINE
32

SCALLOP AND LEEK PARCEL
WITH A TOMATO RISOTTO
34

TIMBALE OF LIGHTLY CURED SALMON AND AVOCADO
WITH A TOMATO AND BASIL DRESSING
40

DEVILLED MACKEREL
WITH A MINT AND TOMATO SALAD
42

DEEP FRIED PRAWN WONTONS
SERVED WITH CHILLI JAM
44

QUANTITIES QUOTED IN THESE RECIPES ARE FOR 4 PEOPLE.

La Coupée

Bruschetta – with garlic brushed ciabatta

300g cherry tomatoes (vine if possible)
4 sun blushed tomatoes
4 tablespoons extra virgin olive oil
16 fresh basil leaves shredded
2 garlic cloves
¼ white onion
8 slices ciabatta
Salt and pepper to taste

Method

~ Cut the cherry tomatoes into quarters, slice the sun blushed tomatoes into strips and finely chop the onion
~ Place the tomatoes and onion in a bowl, add the olive oil and shredded basil and mix well, season with salt and pepper to taste
~ Lightly toast the slices of ciabatta
~ Gently rub the garlic over the toasted ciabatta
~ When ready to serve, place the tomato mix over the ciabatta, drizzle a little balsamic vinegar and basil oil around

HOT CRAB AND BOURSIN TARTLETS

PASTRY

225g of plain flour
65g of butter
1½ tablespoons of cold water
½ teaspoon of salt
65g of lard
1 egg white

METHOD

~ Sieve the flour and the salt into a food processor, add the butter and lard cut into small pieces and process the mixture until it looks like fine breadcrumbs
~ Pour into a large mixing bowl and stir in the water until everything starts to stick together
~ Bring together into a small ball and put it onto a work surface lightly dusted with flour
~ Knead once or twice until smooth, then roll out the pastry and use to line 4 small shallow loose-based tartlet tins (approximately 11cm)
~ Chill for 20 minutes
~ Pre-heat the oven to 220°C
~ Line the pastry cases with greaseproof paper and cover the base with baking beans
~ Bake blind for 15 minutes, then remove the paper and beans and brush the inside of each pastry case with a little unbeaten egg white, return to the oven for a further 2 minutes
~ Remove from the oven and lower the temperature to 200°C

CRAB MIX

280g fresh picked white crab meat
2 egg yolks
90ml of double cream
50g of garlic and chive Boursin cheese
A pinch of cayenne pepper
Salt and pepper

METHOD

~ Mix the crab meat with the egg yolk, cream, cayenne pepper, salt and pepper
~ Spoon the mixture into the pastry tartlets and sprinkle the Boursin cheese on top
~ Bake in the oven for approximately 15–20 minutes until golden brown

Serve with a dressed seasonal salad

Moules Marinière

2kg of fresh mussels
1 medium size onion diced
30g of unsalted butter
2 cloves of garlic
3 tablespoons of chopped parsley
130ml white wine
200ml cream

Method

~ Cleaning the mussels
  Discard any unopened mussels. Wash the mussels in plenty of cold
  water and scrub the shells with a stiff brush, use a knife to scrape
  away any barnacles that may stick to them. Discard any mussels
  that don't close when lightly tapped
~ Fry the onion, butter and garlic in a large saucepan until the
  onion is soft
~ Add the cleaned mussels and white wine, a quick stir and then put
  a tight fitting lid on the pan and let the mussels steam open, this
  should take approximately 5–10 minutes
~ Add the chopped parsley and cream, stir and bring to the boil.
  Discard any unopened mussels before serving

Serve with crusty French bread

How to prepare Moules Mariniere

Fry the onion, butter and garlic in a large saucepan until the onion is soft

Add the cleaned mussels and white wine, a quick stir and then put a tight fitting lid on the pan and let the mussels steam open, this should take approximately 5–10 minutes

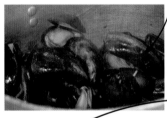

Add the chopped parsley and cream, stir and bring to the boil

Oysters A la Florentine

12 fresh oysters
60g butter
40g plain flour
500ml warm milk
70g grated, Gruyere cheese
2 egg yolks
200g spinach
Freshly chopped parsley
Salt and pepper to season

Method

~ Open the oysters with an oyster knife, lightly wash them and leave aside to drain
~ Heat up a wok until it's smoky. Add a little vegetable oil and quickly toss the spinach in until it has wilted, lightly season with salt and pepper and add 20g of melted butter
~ Melt 40g of the butter in a heavy based saucepan. Add the flour and mix until it's smooth. Add a small amount of warm milk, then add faster until you get a nice creamy white sauce
~ Take the white sauce off the heat and whisk in the egg yolks, then the cheese until smoothly blended. Season this Mornay sauce with salt and pepper and chopped parsley to taste
~ Take the oyster out of the shell, put a small portion of spinach into the shell and put the oyster back on top. Then cover with the Mornay sauce and lightly grill until browned

Serve with salad and a wedge of lemon

Scallop and Leek parcel with a tomato risotto

12 fresh scallops
250g risotto rice
½ small onion diced
150ml white wine
300ml water
8 firm red tomatoes (peeled and diced)
1 leek
20ml balsamic vinegar
30g brown sugar
2 sprigs fresh tarragon
Salt and pepper to season

Method

~ Put a large pan of water on to boil
~ Cut the leek lengthways so you are left with long strips, then blanche in the boiling water for 10 seconds and refresh straight away with iced cold water
~ Cook the onion in a little oil until soft, then add the rice, keep stirring, then add the white wine and cook until it has been absorbed
~ Turn down the heat and add the water a little at a time until the risotto is rich and creamy
~ Place the tomatoes in a pan with the balsamic vinegar and the sugar, cook and reduce until it is a thick red puree, then take off the heat
~ Strain the leek, season the scallops and then gently wrap each scallop with the leek, leaving the roe pointing outwards
~ Add a little butter to a pan and heat, add the wrapped scallops and brown each side
~ Place the scallops in a hot oven for 4 minutes
~ Bring the risotto back to heat and add the tomato puree, chopped tarragon and season to taste

Arrange risotto on heated plates, put 3 scallops each and garnish with crispy pancetta

How to prepare Scallop and Leek parcel with a tomato risotto

Put a large pan of water on to boil, blanche the leeks and refresh in ice cold water

Cook the onion in a little oil until soft, then add the rice, keep stirring, then add the white wine and cook until it has beeen absorbed

Turn down the heat and add the water a little at a time until the risotto is rich and creamy

Place the tomatoes in a pan with the balsamic vinegar and the sugar, cook and reduce until it is a thick red puree, then take off the heat

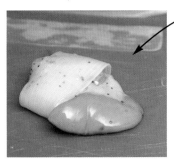

Strain the leek, season the scallops and then gently wrap each scallop with the leek, leaving the roe pointing outwards

Iɴ Tʜᴇ Kɪᴛᴄʜᴇɴ

Timbale of lightly cured Salmon and Avocado – with a tomato and basil dressing

400g salmon fillet, skinned and boned

100g smoked salmon

1 large garlic clove, finely chopped

3 shallots, finely chopped

1½ tablespoons of lemon juice

½ teaspoon of salt

10 turns from a black pepper mill

A pinch of cayenne pepper

A few drops of Worcestershire sauce

2 small avocados

Salad leaves to garnish

Method

~ Thinly slice the salmon fillet and smoked salmon
~ Place them into a bowl with the garlic, shallots, lemon juice, salt, black pepper, cayenne pepper and Worcestershire sauce, mix them well together
~ Peel and cut the avocados in half, cut each half into thin slices and then mix with lemon juice and a pinch of salt
~ Place 4 pastry mould rings in the centre of each plate and layer the salmon inside the ring followed by a layer of avocado, lightly level the top and carefully remove the rings

The Dressing

50ml of extra virgin olive oil

1 tablespoon of lemon juice

2 tomatoes, skinned, seeded and finely diced

½ teaspoon of course sea salt

8 basil leaves very finely shredded

A few pinches of cracked black pepper

~ Lightly mix the dressing ingredients together in a bowl, arrange the salad leaves around each timbale and then spoon the dressing onto the leaves and serve

Devilled Mackerel – with a mint and tomato Salad

4 350g mackerel, cleaned and trimmed

40g of butter

1 teaspoon of caster sugar

1 teaspoon of English mustard powder

1 teaspoon cayenne pepper

1 teaspoon paprika

1 teaspoon ground coriander

2 tablespoons of red wine vinegar

1 teaspoon of fresh ground black pepper

For the mint and tomato salad:

225g of vine-ripened tomatoes sliced

1 small onion, halved and very thinly sliced

1 tablespoon of chopped fresh mint

1 tablespoon of fresh lemon juice

2 teaspoons of salt

Method

~ Pre-heat the grill on high, score each fish with a sharp knife at 1cm intervals on both sides, taking care not to cut too deeply into the flesh

~ Melt the butter in a shallow flame proof dish or roasting tin then remove from the heat

~ Stir in the sugar, mustard, spices, vinegar, salt and pepper, mix well and then add the fish to the butter, turn over once or twice until the fish is well coated while spreading the mixture into the cavity of each fish

~ Transfer the fish to a lightly-oiled baking sheet and grill for 4 minutes on each side until cooked through

~ Meanwhile, layer the sliced tomato, onion and mint on 4 serving plates and sprinkle the layers with fresh lemon juice and seasoning

Place the cooked mackerel with the salad and serve (add a few sautéed slices of potato if you wish)

Deep Fried Prawn Wontons – served with chilli jam

20 raw unshelled headless prawns
20 Chinese wonton pastry squares
50ml of sunflower oil
15g of finely chopped garlic
15g of finely chopped root ginger
225g of finely chopped onion
5 large red chillies seeded and finely chopped
100ml of red wine vinegar
25ml of soy sauce
½ teaspoon of ground star anise
15g of palm sugar or muscovado sugar

Method

~ Peel the prawns, leaving the tail segment and keeping the shells
~ Heat the sunflower oil for the jam, add the prawn shells and fry
  for 1–2 minutes until the shells are crisp
~ Tip the oil and shells through a sieve over a small pan and press
  well to remove all the oil which should be pleasantly flavored by
  the prawns
~ To make the jam, reheat the oil and add the garlic and ginger and
  fry quickly until both are beginning to show colour
~ Add the onion and chilli and fry fiercely for 3–4 minutes, stir in
  vinegar, soy sauce, star anise, sugar and salt
~ Bring to the boil and simmer for 20–30 minutes until the onion
  is very soft and the jam is well reduced and thick, leave jam to
  cool
~ Wrap each prawn in one wonton pastry leaving the tail end
  uncovered and seal with a little water using your fingertip
~ Deep fry the wontons at 190°C for about 1–1½ minutes until
  crisp and golden – lift out and drain on a piece of kitchen paper.

Serve hot with the chilli jam

MAIN COURSES

SEAFOOD MARINIÈRE
WITH ROASTED SALMON, PRAWNS AND CLAMS
48

WHOLE BAKED DOVER SOLE
50

HALF LOBSTER GRILLED
WITH LEMON BUTTER
54

POACHED SALMON
WITH MUSSELS, SPINACH AND CHERVIL
56

RED MULLET EN PAUPIETTE
WITH A CHERRY TOMATO, BLACK OLIVE AND CHILLI SALAD
58

LEMON SOLE VERONIQUE
62

SCALLOPS
64

PAN FRIED SQUID SALAD
WITH A SWEET CHILLI AND LIME DRESSING
66

QUANTITIES QUOTED IN THESE RECIPES ARE FOR 1 PEOPLE.

Honeysuckle above Dixcart Bay

Seafood Marinière – with roasted salmon, prawns and clams

350g of linguine pasta
400g piece of salmon
300g cooked shelled baby prawns
70g butter
6 cloves of garlic finely chopped
2 dessert spoons of chopped parsley
1kg of cleaned clams
½ an onion finely chopped
250ml of white wine
500ml of double cream
Sprigs of fennel to garnish

Method

~ In a large pot filled ¾ full with water, bring to the boil, add a little salt. Place the pasta into the boiling water for about 10–12 minutes, refresh pasta in cold water. Drain and toss with a little olive oil to prevent pasta sticking together
~ To make the garlic butter, soften the butter and mix well with the finely chopped garlic, mix in a little chopped parsley and place back into fridge until needed
~ Pre-heat oven to 200°C
~ Season the salmon with salt and pepper, add a little garlic butter and parsley and then roast in the oven for 15 minutes
~ Place the onion and garlic butter in a large pot on a moderate heat and stir until the onion is soft
~ Place the clams into the pot and stir well
~ Pour in the white wine and cover with a lid to steam the clams open
~ Now add the prawns and flake the salmon into the pot as well
~ Add cream and heat thoroughly, season with salt and pepper
~ In a separate pot re-heat the pasta in boiling water, then drain well and separate into 4 separate bowls

Spoon the seafood sauce over the pasta and finish with freshly chopped parsley

WHOLE BAKED DOVER SOLE

4 Dover soles
125g butter
½ pint of white wine
Chopped parsley
1 sliced lemon
Juice of 1 lemon
4 tablespoons of capers
A little olive oil
Salt and pepper

METHOD

~ Pre-heat oven to 180°C
~ Lightly oil a baking tray
~ Place the Dover soles, skinned side up on the tray and season with a little salt and pepper
~ Place slices of butter over the fish
~ Pour the white wine and sprinkle the capers over the fish
~ Pour the lemon juice and arrange slices of lemon over each fish
~ Place in the pre-heated oven for about 15–20 minutes, until the fish is firm to touch

When the fish is cooked, remove from the oven and place onto the plate, sprinkle with freshly-chopped parsley and serve with buttered new potatoes

How to prepare Dover Sole

Trim the fish by snipping off the fins with sharp kitchen scissors

With a sharp filleting knife make an incision from the tail end under the skin working the knife out to the side

Gently peel back the skin using the knife blade to guide the skin off

Peel the skin back to the head of the fish then trim around with scissors

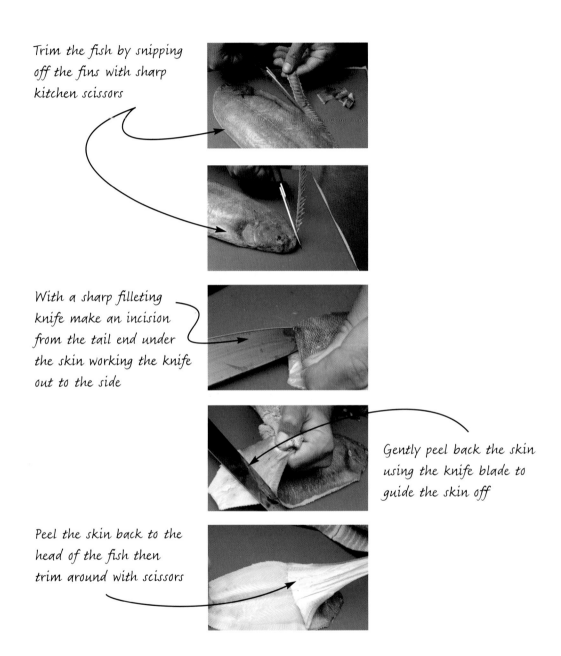

HALF LOBSTER GRILLED WITH LEMON BUTTER

2 good sized lobsters (cooked, halved and cleaned. Your fishmonger
will do this if you wish)
200g of cooked peeled baby prawns
200g of butter (thinly sliced)
Juice from 1 lemon
1 lemon cut into thin slices
2 dessert spoons of chopped parsley
1 small cup of white wine

METHOD

~ Place the half lobsters on a tray, fill the head of the lobsters with
  prawns
~ Arrange the sliced butter and sliced lemon over each lobster half
~ Pour the white wine and the lemon juice over the lobsters
~ Sprinkle the chopped parsley over the lobsters
~ Cover with tinfoil
~ Place in the oven for 10–15 minutes
~ Remove from the oven, remove tinfoil then place under the grill
  for a few minutes

Serve with a crisp salad and garnish with shell-on prawns

POACHED SALMON – WITH MUSSELS, SPINACH AND CHERVIL

4 180g salmon fillets, unskinned
150ml water
150g butter
1 shallot, finely chopped
1 pint of cleaned fresh mussels
900g fresh spinach leaves
1 tablespoon malt whisky
1 teaspoon lemon juice
1 teaspoon chopped chervil
Salt and pepper

METHOD

~ Heat 25g of the butter
~ Add the shallots and cook gently for 3 minutes until soft
~ Meanwhile put the mussels into a large pan of water and cook on high until they have steamed open (see page 30). When they have cooled remove the mussels from shells (leaving approx 8 with shells for garnish)
~ Add the salmon, skin side up to the shallots and add some of the mussel juice, cover and simmer gently for approx 4 minutes. Remove from the heat and then set aside for a further 4 minutes to continue cooking
~ Add 25g of butter to a separate pan and melt, then add the spinach, stir on a high heat until it has wilted and all the excess liquid has evaporated. Season to taste
~ Divide the spinach over 4 warm plates and place the salmon on top
~ Returning to the shallots, reheat and add the whisky and lemon juice, boil for 30 seconds then add the mussels and chervil

Spoon the sauce and mussels over the spinach and salmon, use the unshelled mussels for garnishing the dish.

RED MULLET EN PAUPIETTE —
WITH A CHERRY TOMATO, BLACK OLIVE AND
CHILLI SALAD

4 250g whole red mullet (cleaned and trimmed)

A small bunch of thyme

120ml of extra virgin olive oil

50ml of dry white wine

Juice from 1 lemon

Sea salt and cracked black pepper

50ml of cold water

450g of vine-ripened cherry tomatoes

½ medium hot red finger chilli (seeded and finely chopped)

1 garlic clove (finely chopped)

50g of good quality pitted black olives

1 tablespoon chopped flat leaf parsley

METHOD

~ Pre-heat the oven to 220°C

~ Season the fish inside and out with salt and pepper and place
  2 sprigs of thyme inside the belly of each fish

~ Cut 4 pieces of 30cm square sheets of tin foil and brush each one
  with the olive oil

~ Place the fish on the foil and bring each side up around the fish
  and crimp it together tightly but leaving the top open slightly

~ Mix the white wine with the water, then pour 2 tablespoons of
  the mix with 2 tablespoons of olive oil and 2 teaspoons of lemon
  juice into each parcel

~ Add the remaining thyme and season with a little more salt and
  pepper, seal each parcel well and place on a large tray. Bake for
  approx 12–15 minutes

~ Meanwhile prepare the salad by scattering the tomatoes, chilli,
  garlic and olives on 4 warm plates and drizzle with olive oil

~ When the fish is cooked serve with the salad, sprinkle over the
  freshly-chopped parsley

Let your guests open their own parcel and enjoy the aroma !!

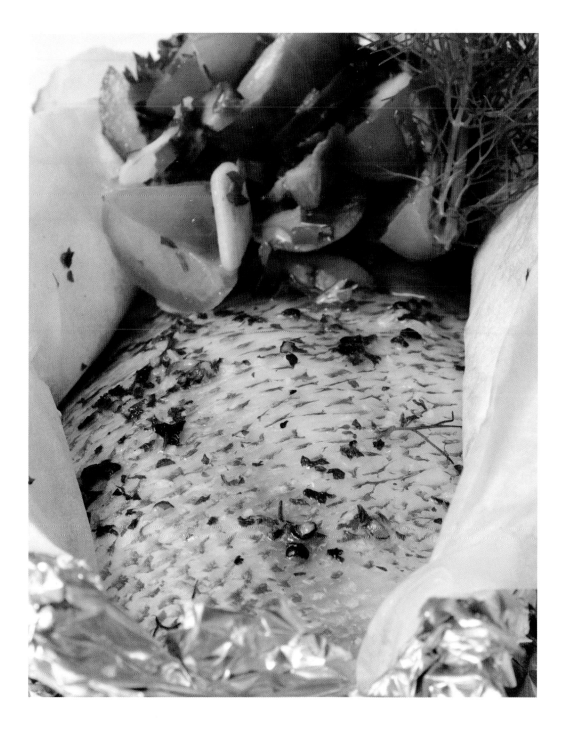

FISH AND FISHERMEN

Clockwise from the top: Opening scallops with the diver, collecting fish at the harbour, oysters and lobster

Above: fresh fish selection. Below: Sark fishermen

61

LEMON SOLE VERONIQUE

4 200g fillets of lemon sole

8 fl oz water

6 fl oz white wine

6 black peppercorns

1 large spring onion (trimmed and sliced)

150g seedless green grapes

Juice of ½ lemon

1 tablespoon butter

2 tablespoons plain flour

2½ fl oz milk

3 tablespoons double cream

2 beaten egg yolks

METHOD

~ Wash the sole fillets and dry on a paper towel

~ Fold each fillet in half and arrange in a well buttered dish

~ Add the water, wine, peppercorns and spring onion

~ Cover the dish with a piece of buttered baking paper, place the dish over a pan of boiling water and steam over moderately high heat for about 12 minutes

~ When cooked, transfer the fish to a warmed serving plate. Cover and keep warm

~ Reserve 10 fl oz of the poaching liquid

~ Peel the grapes and cut in half, sprinkle them with lemon juice and set aside

~ Melt butter in a pan, add flour and mix well, then pour in the milk and the reserved liquid from poaching

~ Whisk until the sauce boils and thickens then remove from the heat

~ Mix together the cream and egg yolks in a separate bowl then add to the sauce

~ Heat and stir continually to prevent the sauce burning

~ Add the grapes

To serve, pour the sauce over the fillets of lemon sole   garnish with a sprig of parsley

SCALLOPS

6-7 large scallops per person
25g butter
2 garlic cloves
1 dessert spoon of chopped parsley
2 slices of crispy pancetta
A little oil to fry the scallops
Salt and pepper to season

METHOD

~ Make a garlic butter by softening the butter and mixing well with
  the finely chopped garlic and the chopped parsley
~ Heat frying pan with a little oil
~ Place each scallop in pan and fry for about a minute, turn each
  one over and fry for a further minute
~ Place the garlic butter in the pan and toss the scallops until the
  butter has melted

Serve straight onto a plate with salad garnish and finish with crispy
pancetta

PAN FRIED SQUID SALAD WITH A SWEET CHILLI AND LIME DRESSING

4 squid tubes cleaned and washed
2 kiwi fruit
4 limes (juice from 2 and the other 2 cut into wedges)
100ml of sweet chilli dipping sauce
200g mixed washed salad leaves
Salt and pepper to taste
Coriander to garnish

METHOD

~ Peel the kiwi fruit and chop to a pulp
~ Cut the squid tubes in half and lightly score the inside of the flesh about 1cm apart then cut into bite size pieces
~ Place the squid into a bowl with the kiwi and mix well, cover with cling film and leave for approximately 2–3 hours in the fridge (this will break down the chewy texture of the squid)
~ Heat a good non-stick pan with a little oil
~ Take the squid pieces and wash away the kiwi fruit, then season with a little salt and pepper
~ Quickly cook the squid pieces by frying on high heat
~ Pour in the sweet chilli sauce and lime juice, bring to the boil and then remove from the heat
~ Arrange the salad leaves between 4 bowls and place the squid on the salad

Garnish with lime wedges and fresh coriander

Fish...Fire...Finesse...

Cooking pancetta and flaming brandy sauce

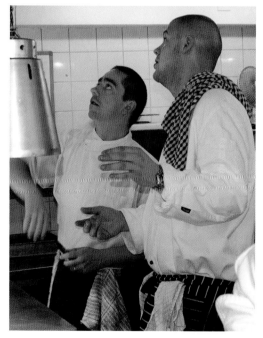

Top: Behind the hot plate during service Bottom: Chef with lobster and checking restaurant orders

OUTSIDE CATERING

DESSERTS

QUANTITIES QUOTED IN THESE RECIPES ARE FOR 4 PEOPLE.

The Island ferry off the north end

INDIVIDUAL BAKED ALASKA

4 pieces of sponge cake (cut into round pieces 6–7 cm in diameter, about 1cm thick)

4 good dessert spoons of any fruit-flavoured coulis

4 scoops of vanilla ice-cream

4 egg whites

225g caster sugar

4 strawberries, thinly sliced

METHOD

~ Neatly arrange the 4 pieces of sponge onto a flat ovenproof tray

~ Spoon over the fruit coulis on to each sponge

~ Arrange the strawberries on top

~ Place a scoop of ice-cream onto each sponge, then place into the freezer

~ Meanwhile whisk the egg whites to a stiff consistency and fold in the sugar to produce a meringue

~ Use the meringue mix to cover the ice-cream and the sponge, neaten with a palate knife and use the remainder of the meringue in a piping bag to cover again making sure you leave no gaps

~ Now place into a pre-heated oven 230°C/250°C

~ Cook until meringue is golden brown on the outside, approximately 4–5 minutes

Dust with icing sugar and serve immediately

ELDERFLOWER PANACOTTA

2½ sheets of gelatin
30g sugar
200ml double cream
40ml milk
150ml elderflower cordial

METHOD

~ Lightly oil 4 ramekins
~ Place milk, cream, sugar and cordial into a saucepan and bring to the boil
~ Soak the gelatin sheets in cold water until soft
~ Add the soaked gelatin to the hot liquid and mix well until dissolved
~ Strain the mix through a sieve into a bowl and place over ice cold water, stirring continually until mix starts to thicken
~ Pour the mix into ramekins and place in the fridge for 2 hours

Garnish with lavender flowers, orange segments and chocolate wafer

Vanilla Crème Brulee

4 egg yolks
40g sugar
400ml cream
2 vanilla pods or 2 teaspoons strong vanilla essence

Method

~ Pre-heat oven to 120°C
~ Pour cream and vanilla into a saucepan and bring to the boil, after boiling remove pods if used
~ Place egg yolks and sugar into a bowl and beat until pale and creamy
~ Pour the hot cream and vanilla liquid into the eggs and mix well
~ Using a ladle, skim off any foam that has appeared
~ Pour the mixture into ramekins
~ Place each ramekin into a deep try and then fill the tray with hot water to half way up the ramekin
~ Place in the oven and cook for 25 minutes
~ Once cooked, remove from tray and immediately chill in a fridge for at least 1 hour

When ready to serve, sprinkle the top with sugar and caramelize with a blow torch and serve with good old shortbread

COFFEE BOMBES WITH A RUM TRUFFLE CENTRE

1 tub of good quality toffee ice-cream
28g cake crumbs
28g ground almonds
56g plain chocolate (chopped)
3 tablespoons double cream
2 tablespoons of rum or brandy

METHOD

~ Put 4 individual 200ml pudding moulds into the freezer to chill
~ Leave the ice-cream at room temperature until soft enough to spread
~ To make the truffle filling, mix the cake crumbs and almonds together in a bowl
~ Put the chocolate and cream into a small bowl and stand over a pan of simmering water and stir until melted
~ Add the chocolate and cream mixture to the crumb mix, add the rum and mix well
~ Spread the softened ice cream around the base and sides of the moulds, leaving a cavity in the centre for the truffle filling – now freeze for 1 hour or until firm
~ Fill each centre with the truffle mixture and level the surface, cover and freeze for at least another 1 hour

To serve, dip the moulds briefly in hot water then carefully take out the bombes and place on to serving plates
To garnish with chocolate leaves:
Using a small paint brush, thinly spread melted chocolate on the under side of a clean leaf (the leaf needs to be dry and undamaged) leave to dry then gently peel away the leaf

Choux Pastry Swans with a Chocolate Fudge Sauce

Ingredients for chocolate fudge sauce

5 tbsp single cream
28g cocoa powder
115g caster sugar
170g golden syrup
28g butter
Pinch of salt
½ teaspoon vanilla essence

Method for chocolate fudge sauce

~ Combine all the ingredients, except the vanilla
  essence, in a saucepan over a low heat and mix well
~ Slowly bring to the boil, stirring for 3–4 minutes,
  then add the vanilla essence
~ Cool the sauce to a warm temperature before serving

Ingredients and method for chantilly cream

285ml of whipping cream (whipped)
~ Sweeten with caster sugar and flavour with a few
  drops of vanilla essence according to taste

Ingredients for pastry

285ml water
Pinch of sugar and salt
115g butter
140g strong flour (sieved)
4 beaten eggs
Icing sugar to dust

METHOD FOR PASTRY

~ Bring the water, sugar and butter to the boil in a saucepan, remove from heat
~ Add the sieved flour and mix in with a wooden spoon
~ Return to low heat and stir continuously until the mixture leaves the side of the pan
~ Remove from heat and allow to cool
~ Gradually add the beaten eggs and mix well
~ The paste should be firm enough to hold its shape
~ Mould into 8 éclair shapes with a piping bag to make the choux buns and place on a lightly-greased baking sheet
~ Bake at 200°C/220°C until they rise and have a good colour. Allow to cool
~ With remaining mix, using a smaller piping bag, make swan heads
~ Bake at 200°C but they will not take long to cook. Be careful not to break them when removing them from the tray. Allow to cool
~ Now cut the top half off each choux bun, for each half cut again length ways with scissors to form the wings
~ Pipe on the whipped chantilly cream to each bottom half of choux bun. After this press in the cut choux bun to form the wings and gently place the swan head between the wing at the lower end
~ Arrange 2 swans on each plate, reheat the chocolate sauce and pour around the swans. Dust with icing sugar and serve

How to prepare Choux Pastry Swans

Mould into 8 éclair shapes with a piping bag to make the choux buns and place on a lightly-greased baking sheet. Bake at 200°C/220°C until they rise and have a good colour. Allow to cool

With remaining mix, using a smaller piping bag, make swan heads. Bake at 200°C but they will not take long to cook. Be careful not to break them when removing them from the tray. Allow to cool

Now cut the top half off each choux bun, for each half cut again length ways with scissors to form the wings

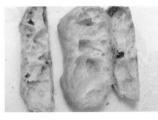

Pipe on the whipped chantilly cream to each bottom half of choux bun. After this press in the cut choux bun to form the wings and gently place the swan head between the wing at the lower end.

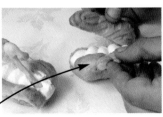

TIA MARIA CHEESECAKE

120g hobnob biscuits
10/20g knob of melted butter
56g caster sugar
2 egg yolks
2½ soaked gelatin sheets (in cold water)
300g of cream cheese
250ml of semi whipped cream
1 or 2 shots of Tia Maria (to taste)
Chocolate pencils and fruit coulis to garnish (you can buy these at good delicatessens)

METHOD

~ Finely crush the biscuits until they are like breadcrumbs, then add butter and mix until the mixture starts to stick together
~ Pour biscuit mix into 4 circular moulds and press hard, trying to level the mix at the bottom. Leave in fridge for around 30 minutes
~ Cream the egg yolks and sugar until white in colour, add cream cheese and mix well
~ Add the soaked gelatin to a little of the cream, warm through until the gelatin has dissolved, then add this liquid to the cream cheese mix
~ Add the Tia Maria then add the semi whipped cream and mix
~ Remove the biscuits from the fridge and pour in the cheesecake mix, then set in the fridge until needed

Garnish with a chocolate pencil, fruit and coulis

White Chocolate Tart

PASTRY

50g icing sugar
100g unsalted butter
300g plain flour
100g cocoa powder
1 egg

CHOCOLATE MIX

195g white chocolate
140ml cream
80ml milk
1 egg

METHOD FOR THE PASTRY

~ Cream the butter and sugar together, then add the flour and cocoa powder and mix until it starts to look like breadcrumbs
~ Add the egg and mix until the pastry comes together
~ Wrap in cling film and place in fridge, leave to rest for about 30 minutes
~ Once out of the fridge, roll onto a floured surface and divide into 4 lined tartlet cases
~ Bake blind for 15 minutes, then take out and leave to rest

METHOD FOR CHOCOLATE MIX

~ Pre-heat oven to 110°C
~ Place milk and cream in a saucepan and bring to the boil
~ Add the white chocolate and stir until melted and mixed thoroughly
~ Lightly beat egg and add to hot mix
~ Distribute mix into 4 individual tartlets and bake in the oven for 15–20 minutes

How to prepare White Chocolate Tart

Wrap in cling film and place in fridge, leave to rest for about 30 minutes

Once out of the fridge, roll onto a floured surface and divide into 4 lined tartlet cases

Bake blind for 15 minutes, then take out and leave to rest

Distribute mix into 4 individual tartlets and bake in the oven for 20–25 minutes

CRÊPES WITH CRÈME PATISSIERE AND BANANA

Ingredients for the crêpes
225g flour
3 eggs
500ml milk

METHOD FOR CRÊPES

~ Put all the ingredients in a food processor and mix till smooth
~ Heat a nonstick pan. Pour in a ladle of mix and by holding handle tip the mix around the pan until thin, then turn once
~ Leave crepes to one side to cool down

Ingredients for the pastry cream
½ pt milk
1 egg
28g flour
7g custard powder
½ vanilla pod
2 large bananas

METHOD FOR THE PASTRY CREAM

~ Beat eggs and sugar and add flour and custard powder
~ Boil milk and add to egg and sugar mix
~ Return to heat and add the vanilla pod
~ Mix till thick, then chill
~ Remove vanilla pod

Ingredients for butterscotch sauce
50g butter
50g golden syrup
50g caster sugar

METHOD FOR BUTTERSCOTCH SAUCE

~ Melt all the ingredients in a saucepan

MAIN METHOD

~ Place crêpe on plate and fill with the pastry cream and sliced bananas (or any other fruit) and fold into a parcel
~ Pour round the butterscotch sauce and sprinkle with the icing sugar
~ Garnish with berries and fresh mint sprig

Encouraging the Future

MAPS
AND MORE

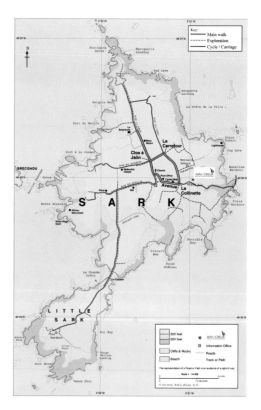

*The Island from the east and
(below) west.*

SARK
CHANNEL ISLANDS
GY9 0SB

TELEPHONE: +44 (0) 1481 832 036
FAX: +44 (0) 1481 832 368
EMAIL: RECEPTION@AVALDUCREUX.CO.UK

ACKNOWLEDGEMENTS

Many thanks to:
Dick Adams – Sark
Our long-standing supplier of the best Local Lobster and Crab
Kevin Laws of "Barbara Kay"– Sark
Responsible for wonderful fresh Bass, Turbot and Brill
Kieran Peree – Sark
local diver who hand selects the scallops
Dave and Hilary Curtis – Sark
Sark new potatoes and fresh vegetables
Dave Scott – Sark
The local shepherd with the best stress-free lamb that you will ever taste
Chris and Mary Nightingale – Sark Dairy Produce
Paul Williams – C.I.B.N. Wholesale, Sark
Glyn Williams – Le Clos Bourel, Sark
Richard Torode and the team at Cimandis – Guernsey
Grant Le Tissier of Manor Farm Foods – Guernsey

KITCHEN TEAM

Head Chef Gary Thompson
Sous Deano Knox

Chef de Partie Jay North
Oysters a la Florentine, Scallops and leek parcels with a tomato riscotto
Junior Chef de Partie Jack Brough

Pastry Jon Denley
Elderflower Panacotta, Vanilla Creme Brulee, White Choc Tart

Commis Ray Pullen
Kitchen Hands Ross O'Donnell, Alan Morgan, Tom Long

Special thanks to Lisa Thompson, Gary's wife and Assistant Manager (at the Hotel) who has put up with many late nights for this book to happen and finally to all the guests who have supported us throughout the years

Photographed and Produced by
Chris Andrews Publications Limited, www.cap-ox.co.uk
Designed by Mike Brain Graphic Design Limited, Oxford
Introduction text by Jo Birch, Sark
Published by
Gateway Publishing Ltd
PO Box 31
Sark GY9 0SG
ISBN 978-1-902471-05-1
Telephone: +44 (0) 1481 832203